MENTAL TOUGHNESS

A Psychologist's Guide to Becoming Psychologically Strong - Develop Resilience, Self-Discipline & Willpower on Demand

KATHERINE CHAMBERS

© Copyright 2018 – **(Katherine Chambers) All rights reserved.**

The contents of this book may not be reproduced, duplicated or transmitted without direct written permission from the author. Under no circumstances will any legal responsibility or blame be held against the publisher for any reparation, damages, or monetary loss due to the information herein, either directly or indirectly.

Legal Notice:

This book is copyright protected. This is only for personal use. You cannot amend, distribute, sell, use, quote or paraphrase any part or the content within this book without the consent of the author.

Disclaimer Notice:

Please note the information contained within this document is for educational and entertainment purposes only. Every attempt has been made to provide accurate, up to date and reliable complete information. No warranties of any kind are expressed or implied. Readers acknowledge that the author is not engaging in the rendering of legal, financial, medical or professional advice. The content of this book has been derived from various sources. Please consult a licensed professional before attempting any techniques outlined in this book.

By reading this document, the reader agrees that under no circumstances are is the author responsible for any losses, direct or indirect, which are incurred as a result of the use of information contained within this document, including, but not limited to, —errors, omissions, or inaccuracies.

TABLE OF CONTENTS

Introduction v

Part 1: High Level Mental Toughness Tendencies 1

Chapter 1: What Does Mental Toughness Actually Entail? 3

Chapter 2: Myths About the Mentally Strong 9

Chapter 3: The 3 R's - Being Resourceful, Resilient & Relentless...17

Chapter 4: Habits Hold the Key to Mental Fortitude ..25

Part 2: Mental Strength - Techniques & Practical Strategies to Naturally Attain It 33

Chapter 5: Freedom From Fear & Surviving Stress 35

Chapter 6: Goal Setting Secrets 43

Chapter 7: Visualization - Mental Imagery IS Mental Toughness 51

Chapter 8: Talking Tools & Conversational Skills
For Greater Grit 59

Conclusion 65

Bonus Chapters 69

INTRODUCTION

I talk a lot about finding your purpose, as its imperative to living a joyful and fulfilling existence. Life is inherently struggle, so you need to find the thing which helps you cultivate desirable psychological strengths. Resilience, persistence and what we commonly think of as willpower, just come as a by product of this work. My true calling is helping others find theirs. This is why I write these books, and this edition might be the icing on the cake when it comes to attaining true mental toughness.

The traditional view is that this requires tough love, grit, and blood, sweat and tears. But does it? If you've never questioned this, you really should. In my opinion, it isn't about having superhuman abilities to overcome struggle, its about surrendering instead. This sounds counterintuitive, but anything which requires effort, won't work by default. In most instances, surrender is the better option, but this sounds like weakness to most people.

Social media constantly preaches about "embracing the grind" or some other equally motivating, but cliched statement. In my experience, willpower in a traditional sense is a myth, its for old wives tales of knights slaying dragons. Yes there are people who experience physically demanding times. But the average person will seldom be exposed to this level of mental and physical training. We require a different strategy to develop psychological resolve.

We simply need the right mental tools to deal with everyday life. It requires an adjustment of attitude, to take full responsibility and control of our feelings and reactions. If you let situations and words dictate your mood, then you're a prisoner to these instances. You're a hostage to anything and everyone around you. Its not about being mentally tough here, but rather letting go of that which trigger negative responses. It takes a re-wiring of the mind, or at least quieting it for the most part.

Its about creating positive habits and putting them into practice in a self-disciplined and consistent fashion. But most importantly, changing your self-imagery, as how you see yourself is paramount. You will naturally handle tough situations if you view yourself as a strong individual. If you see yourself as weak, that is how you will react. This works in all walks of life.

Experiences will change, but the rules of the game remain the same. You can see it everyday. Two people will get into an altercation like a car accident, one will ponder it for weeks, whilst the other forgets the incident almost immediately. Its the same situation and severity for both. But one experiences a big effect, whilst the other almost none. What has changed? Simply their outlook, how they perceived the situation.

My favorite fable which describes this concept best, is the story of the two frogs, which goes something like this. Once there was a group of frogs who used to play by a big ditch. Most of the frogs took care when passing this pit. Although one day, two younger and more playful members, got a little too close to the edge and fell in. The walls were so high, they resigned themselves to never getting out. Although, both began to relentlessly jump and hop in the hope of doing so.

All of their froggy friends would gather round and shout down "Its no good, its to high, you'll never get out". "Don't waste your energy, you'll never make it". Whilst this was tragic advice, it was technically true. They should have followed the beaten path after all. So after struggling endlessly for days trying to jump out, one of the frogs began to let this fate sink in. He believed an escape couldn't be done, and collapsed in a heap as he took his last breaths.

The second frog kept going though. He didn't give up, and whilst attempting one last time, miraculously managed to grasp the edge and pull himself out. Everyone exclaimed, "Why did you not give up? How did you know you could get out?" Exhausted he looked up whilst lipreading their remarks, and replied "I'm deaf, when I saw you all shouting down, I thought you were cheering me on, which gave me the strength to continue…"

Be extremely careful what you're allowing into your mind, and how you're interpreting it. Perceptions dictate everything, from insecurities and self-conscious behavior, to intentional success seeking traits. Ensure you're instilling the right ones in yourself.

My aim is to help you do just that. Teach you the mental techniques to develop true psychological strength in the most efficient way. To turn you into the second frog, just without the struggle.

PART 1: HIGH LEVEL MENTAL TOUGHNESS TENDENCIES

CHAPTER 1: WHAT DOES MENTAL TOUGHNESS ACTUALLY ENTAIL?

"Physical strength measures WHAT you can do. Mental strength measures whether you'll actually do it"

(Tim Grover)

I'm frequently asked what I believe to be the key ingredients which make for optimal performance in any endeavor. These include the various academic and athletic activities for the most part. In truth, people already know the answer to this question. We all know that it takes a combination of both natural, physical ability, in addition to the mental capacity and drive to achieve success. This is acutely true for top level athletes, but the same can be said for being a great business leader or excellent parent for instance. The same rules apply. So the question really is, what percentage of these factors produces the best results?

Its no surprise that the person who is the most naturally "gifted" will typically come out ahead. Although when these innate abilities are closely matched, the person with the right mindset will win every time. This is because the most in-depth studies show that physical talent and skill, only account for around 30% of peak performance. That leaves a whopping 70% for mindset and work ethic! A lot of ground can be made up with the correct thinking patterns and application in this sense.

I certainly don't doubt the impact our cognitive capabilities have over our real life results. My entire academic and working life has been dedicated to uncovering the most efficient psychological techniques and strategies in this regard. However, as I have already stated, I do not hold a main stream view on mental toughness. Why? I have simply seen it fail on too many occasions. Or work for a short period of time, but ultimately let the person down when it matters most. Short bursts of motivational activity or mental "grit" will fizzle out before long.

This is the official definition of mental toughness which everyone clings onto. It's the measure of individual resilience and confidence which can predict success in sport, education, workplace or any endeavor for that matter. I actually don't disagree with this entirely, as I do think resilience is an extremely important factor in terms of what a person will get out of life. But its how we get there which counts. I believe its achieved in a different way than you might imagine. Its not acquired through constant effort and struggle, but rather surrender. But more on this later.

Lessons From the Military

We traditionally get our notions on mental toughness from the professional service men and women around the world. These individuals have to attain high levels of mental and physical strength as must, not by choice. Brutal training regiments and boot camps are designed to push army, air force and navy cadets to the limit. To test their physical and mental capabilities, and continually push through them. These training camps are designed to break people down. To take their bodies, and more importantly the mind, to places they haven't been before. So when faced with similar situations in the field, they can handle them with ease.

"We don't rise to the level of our expectations. We fall to the level of our training."

(Archilochus)

This seems to confirm the studies I've already suggested, that the physical attributes, like speed, strength and cardiovascular endurance, aren't the things which determine results the most. Its the individuals ability to persist through the pain, in essence, its those with the greatest mental toughness who come out ahead. Its the ability to pick the body up and move it, even though you feel there's noting left in the tank.

Retired Navy Seal and ultra-endurance athlete David Goggins, is famous for stating that at the point of complete and utter physical exhaustion, the body is only around 50% of max output. Its up to the mind to push the arms and legs to squeeze out the additional 50% of potential. But very few of us will ever experience this level of physical training in reality. That's not to say we can't employ the same tactics to a lesser, more manageable degree. I am a big proponent of continually pushing yourself to expand the perimeters of your comfort zone.

My work has been focused on how best to do this for the everyday individual. In reality, its about defining what mental toughness means to the average person on the street. Pinpointing what it entails for you. This can be any variation of factors which may or may not include any of the following:

- Completing work or college assignments on time
- Meditating for 30 minutes everyday
- Working out 4 days a week for an entire month
- Spending an hour with your kids each morning before school

It doesn't matter what this maybe for you, you simply have to clearly define them. Mental toughness starts within the mind. It begins with the mental fortitude to get something done. But it also requires subsequent physical effort to complete the task or activity. Only then can you confirm its accomplishment. This requires definite action steps and goals to achieve. As we'll see later on, this comes through changing ingrained thought patterns and developing better habits by and large.

It entails changing the mental picture of yourself, visualizing the person who can get these things done with ease. This is how you achieve mental toughness without struggle. That is how you get the most done with minimal effort. I'm certainly not adverse to grafting hard when its required, but it just doesn't work when trying to overcome hurdles in your mind. For this, you need to follow the path of least resistance, and this comes from surrender.

This is the big lie we are fed in society. We are told that it takes 80 hour work weeks of blood, sweat and tears to get anything of significance done. Although, if you have ever witnessed truly high performance people at work, they seem to accomplish everything almost effortlessly. That is because they are not continually tripping themselves up in their mind. They have simply made the necessary adjustments in their thinking to produce the results they are getting. Hard work for hard works sake is a myth. If you are unsure of this, the following chapter will highlight some more examples to demonstrate this point more clearly.

CHAPTER 2: MYTHS ABOUT THE MENTALLY STRONG

"You have power over your mind, not outside events. Realize this, and you will find strength"

(Marcus Aurelius)

So now that we've seen what mental toughness traditionally encompasses, its time to take a look at some more myths about mentality strong people. The common thought is that these folks somehow possess superhuman courage. That is not the case. In extreme instances such as the military personnel or high levels athletes, this maybe true. These individuals have certainly trained both mentally and physically to develop what seems like extraterrestrial capabilities.

But for the everyday person, they have simply changed their outlook on life. They have made a decision that they can handle whatever comes their way, and just get on with it. This section could easily be titled "Attitude Determines Altitude" or "Persistence is the Key to Success", or my personal favourite "Just bloody do it!" In this sense, success is achieved by simply showing up. By putting in the work each day, not by continually overcoming insurmountable odds. Its small, consistent, incremental wins that we are looking for. Not scaling Everest each week!

I have talked in much greater detail about finding your purpose in previous books, so I'll save you the explanation again here. But needless to say that its a crucial thing to find. Then whatever you are trying to achieve won't feel like work. It will simply be doing what you were put on this planet to do I.e. to actualize and manifest these goals into your physical reality. Then things will become dramatically easier by default.

Human beings are creative creatures by very nature. We want to work towards achieving milestones and are happiest when on the path to doing so. This is how our cognitive mechanisms were designed to function. There are countless people I've counseled over the years who suddenly experience a sudden drop in confidence, or even full on existential crisis's. Its almost always due to having achieved something big, such as the dream job or high level sporting goal. These folks were laser driven whilst on the road to accomplishing these feats, but are now somewhat lost. They have reached the top of the mountain with nowhere else to go. All I get them to do is re-evaluate things and get a new goal. This reinvigorates them without exception.

The Australian shepherd dog is a prime example of this. Its a very hyperactive breed which requires high amounts of exercise and activity to keep it happy. In fact, it will start to go crazy if there are no animals to herd. Owners report that the dog will endlessly run rings around the house, or dig holes in the yard in the absence of any meaningful work. Humans are very similar in this sense, we need focus and direction towards a worthy task in order to keep us happy and functioning well.

In addition to this, too many of us focus on the "how" something should be done, not "what" should be done. Everyone's heard the adage that if your "why" is big enough, then you'll find the "how to". Through fear of sounding like an esoteric law of attraction guru, I couldn't agree more. I'll expand on this greater within the chapter on goal setting. But for now, lets just say its wise to focus on the process, which requires the following two principles.

1. Persistence Equals Results

> "The wise man is concerned only with the purpose of his actions, not their outcomes; beginnings are within our power, but the outcome is ultimately up to fortune".
>
> (Seneca)

Again, results don't come from mere contemplation alone. It takes action, a lot of action. This is where most people trip themselves up when it comes to mental toughness. They get a momentary burst of motivation, but give up on a new venture or activity at the first or second sign of trouble. But the magic comes from persisting past these set-backs. It lies on the other side of these hurdles.

Oil companies don't make money by continually drilling shallow holes. They do their research and calculations, and drill a well deep enough until they hit the oil deposits. Those who benefited most from the mid-west gold rush did so by drilling until they eventually hit the vein they were aiming for, not stopping "3 feet from gold". It's as though our existence on this earth has been set up solely to test the will of human beings. To reward those with the persistence to push through problems.

In essence, you have to be a dolphin. Look around, make a plan, and be decisive about the direction you want to go in. Then dive and swim and swim for 6 months before eventually surfacing for air to re-evaluate things. Then after some adjustments, dive and swim again! I appreciate this is easier said then done in today's fast moving world with untold amounts of distractions. But you will be amazed at how much you will be able to achieve by sticking to this simple productivity principle.

So just get on with ploughing for your goals without distractions and you'll be just fine. We do need to make the distinction between being busy and being productive though. It's pointless to fill up your day with activity for activities sake. Remember that working hard as a means to an end is a myth. You've heard the saying that "If you want something done, then give it to a busy person." I would argue you should give it to the productive person. These people are conditioned to get results, not just fit a lot into their day. They have trained themselves to achieve a certain amount of output, so adding just one more activity is of little disruption.

Everyone has this innate drive and persistent hunger within them. It's not until we see the rest of society making excuses for why things aren't working out, and justifications for throwing in the towel, that we do the same. It takes a mental switch and much daily practice to become a mentally strong and driven person again. I get more done in a day then anyone I know. But I still frequently feel lazy and bogged down. It takes a conscious effort to recognize these instances and to reaffirm my purpose in order to snap back into the correct state for action. Once you do this enough times, your identity begins to change from a person who gets moderate amounts of activity done, to getting everything and anything done! You simply need to increase your activity thermostat and persist through momentary set-backs.

2. Excuses are the Enemy

I always find it interesting how most people will show up on time for arrangement's with others. They will turn up 20 minutes early for a doctors appointment or business meeting, but half an hour late for a workout or study session they have scheduled for themselves. I'm certainly not suggesting you begin wasting other peoples time, but simply start respecting your own to the same degree. And this entails not making any excuses.

Doing so will ensure you take maximum responsibility for yourself and your actions. Nobody is going to take care of your own success for you. Whether this is in business, academia or within the family setting. All of these areas require work which only you can do. Again, military personnel will have an advantage here, as they are all too aware of the importance of self-sufficiency and extreme ownership of responsibility. Excuses will just not cut it in their world.

But even within general everyday life, you learn that excuses aren't relevant anymore, results are the only thing which matters. Yes there will be reasons why something happened or didn't go your way. You were over looked for that promotion because your boss prefers your colleague who he/she socializes with. Or you got turned down for that date because you weren't smart or good looking enough.

If you allow these things to dictate why something did or did not happen to you, then you are powerless to fix them. That is really what we are getting at here. Become so invaluable that your boss has no choice but to promote you. Become so eligible that every single person in town is knocking down your door to take you out.

It's not denying reality or beating yourself up for no reason. It's a mindset which is simply the most beneficial for you to adopt. If everything is within your control, and your responsibility to fix, then the ultimate power lies with you. You become the driving force in your own life. You decide your circumstances. In essence, you now have complete control over your future, and can steer the ship in any direction you wish.

It's my opinion that every major psychological growth spurt in life, is preceded by a definite and conscious choice to assume more responsibility. It might be taking that promotion which requires handling more staff, having a child or up-sizing your home. Each of these instances takes an upgrade in the cognitive work you must perform to ensure you can handle the responsibility, and adequately deal with an expansion of your comfort zone. However, when you are fully committed to persistent action towards your true purpose, your creative faculties will take care of the rest. You will find a way around any problem as your desire is big enough to solve it. Excuses will simply not enter into the equation.

Progress in life will always cause additional and bigger problems to arise. Its the surest sign you are heading on the right path to growth. This is the crux of mental toughness I.e. learning how to deal with these difficulties with increasing competence and confidence. It doesn't take superpowers. The mentally strong are everyday individuals who have just learned how to get it done. If you want some additional pointers on how to cultivate this within yourself, than the following chapter will show you how.

CHAPTER 3: THE 3 R'S - BEING RESOURCEFUL, RESILIENT & RELENTLESS

I know what you're thinking. These 3 R's are just self-help buzz words which begin with the same letter of the alphabet. In some regards, this is true. But I really do believe that these traits are the three attributes required for building mental strength in the traditional sense. In reality, these could be called the 3 P's I.e. being a Problem Solver, Pragmatic & Perseverant. This would be describing the same qualities by and large. So lets take a look at each more closely.

1. Resourcefulness

In truth, being resourceful and a problem solver is the very essence of being a self-starter or entrepreneur. Its simply about becoming creative, especially when you have very little or nothing when formulating a plan. But never be afraid of small beginnings, this is how everything starts. Facebook was born in a Harvard dorm room, Apple within a garage. We often get fixated on the end of these success stories. We fail to see the initial struggles, when each of these founders had to get wildly creative in the beginning.

I myself didn't come from a place of privilege. My grandparents moved to the US from Europe during the early 1900's. They certainly had an immigrant mindset in terms of work ethic. They took nothing for granted and instilled the same within my parents, and eventually me. They constantly preached the notion that anything could be worked out if you thought long and hard enough about the problem. If you tried to fit enough pieces of the puzzle together, you will eventually complete the picture.

Even though I studied a vast array of psychological principles during my academic life. I still attribute much of my real world and business success, to this resourcefulness mindset my grandparents bestowed upon me. I was essentially trained to think outside the box for solutions, and not to become disheartened when the first, second or third attempt failed to work. It's insanely more easy with the help of the internet today. You can find virtual freelancers to perform literally any task you need from any location in the world. I used to do it the old school way, by picking up the phone or pounding the pavements going from meeting to meeting. Now you can switch on a laptop and send a few emails, or log into linkedIn, and you have all the resources you need at your very finger tips.

2. Developing Resilience

Its also no secret that most of us live pampered lives in today's day and age. We don't have it perfect, but we have much more compared to what our ancestors had in terms of basic amenities and comfort. Everyone reading this will almost certainly have a roof over their head, adequate clothing, and 3 square meals at the very least. Its likely that you will have central heating and/or air conditioning too. None of which were afforded to King's and Queen's just 500 years ago.

One of the ways I've found to give yourself an added boost of resilience, is to forego some of these comforts for a handful of days per month. To take a cold shower once in a while or sleep on the floor. Live as frugally as possible, eating only the cheapest food and wearing coarse clothing. You'll soon realize that you can endure these discomforts far easier than you'd anticipated. I recommend doing this regularly, and for as long as possible in order to test your character, and not just as a diversion from the monotony of daily life. Performing this exercise serves as a means to toughen yourself, so when faced with a genuinely difficult situation, you can handle it without incident.

Much like the military personnel I previously described, performing this exercise is like a soldier preparing for battle during peacetime. So when they are called upon for active service, they are able to perform their duty without hindrance. By becoming familiar with what it means to "live rough" once in a while, you remind yourself that you can endure much more than you realize. That the obstacles you face in everyday life are momentary discomforts which can be overcome easily.

Another mental exercise we can use to develop resilience, is to imagine losing something or someone we view as extremely important to us. I have wrote about this catastophizing method in more detail within *"Self-Esteem For Women: A Psychologists Guide"*. We can essentially rob present troubles of their power, simply by anticipating and working through them beforehand. I find this mental exercise helps when anticipating some significant up coming event, like starting a new business or moving house.

By visualizing the worst case scenarios beforehand, you can prevent yourself from becoming paralyzed by fear, as you know that you can handle any major issues if they do arise. This isn't the same as dwelling on potential problems. You do not want to do this as you will likely bring them into existence more readily by doing so. But rather, its about pragmatically looking at the situation and devising a plan for anything which could go wrong. Once you have done this, there is no point in worrying for one second longer. Just get on with your day with increased peace of mind.

This technique is intended to alleviate anxiety resulting from perceived future events, essentially when blowing things out of proportion. For example, an employee may worry that by making a small mistake at work, could result in them being let go. Thus, the way to challenge these irrational thoughts is essentially to play a game of "what if?" What if I did lose my job? What if I did make the mistake? What's the worse that could happen? What would I do next? The purpose of asking and answering these questions is to help you deal with the outcome and assure you that, even if the worst does happen, its not the end of the world. You will realize that you can survive and even prevail through the worst case scenario.

Our goal should be to become like the "headland", where the waves constantly break, but which still stands firm, even though the foaming waters churn around it. Instead of saying, "It's my bad luck that something bad has occurred". Rather state "Although this has happened to me, its my good luck that I can bear it without becoming distressed, neither being beaten by the present nor afraid of the future". In other words, don't wish for an easy life. Wish for the strength to endure a testing one.

3. Be Relentless

"Never, never, never give up"

(Winston Churchill)

As always, if you have a worthwhile purpose driven goal you are striving for, this should be much less of an issue. You still need to light the fire every now and then. To remind yourself why you are getting out of bed to do what you are doing each day. But true inspiration is the perfect fuel for tireless effort anyway. Which is why you desperately need to find this true calling. Otherwise you will just get caught up trying things and getting constantly burnt out in the process.

Most people get trapped in the illusion of progress, they are just busy doing activities. You need to really assess whether these things are truly taking you to another level of progress. It could be argued that all activities are developing you in some ways, as you are learning from the experience. There is some truth to this. But the reality is that most people are simply spinning their wheels doing the same old thing, and expecting different results, the very definition of insanity. Don't waste the prime years of your life treading water, only to find that a decade down the line you are no further on in your achievements. This is true in a financial sense, but more importantly in terms of genuine growth and responsibility.

If I'm being honest, I believe this third trait I.e. being relentless/persistent is the one secret to success. I know this is a simplification, but if you do something for long enough and without giving up, you'll eventually figure out how to get where you are going. You will certainly feel some pain as you go, but you will course correct using the previous two principles I.e. with resourcefulness and resilience. You can vastly smooth your trajectory and quicken the process by learning from mistakes in this way.

So in reality, each of these three elements are essential for creating success in their own way. Mental toughness just comes as a by product of the work you had to put in to acquire them. Your character will be chiseled as a result of the trail and error along the way. You'll garner a great deal from the set-backs you'll face, but more importantly, using one (or more) of these principles to over come them.

Some would argue that its the other way around. That you need to develop mental strength first. Only then is it possible to be resourceful, resilient and relentless. In truth, its a bit of a chicken and egg situation. However, I do think you need just a spark of inspiration to begin whatever you are attempting. But true psychological strength will ultimately come from the experience of doing it, and by seeing that whatever you are attempting, really isn't that difficult after all.

CHAPTER 4: HABITS HOLD THE KEY TO MENTAL FORTITUDE

"We are what we repeatedly do. Excellence then, is not an act, but a habit"

(Aristotle)

If there is one central theme throughout all of my work, it is this. Changing your circumstances in life comes down to doing two things. Firstly, by adjusting your thinking patterns and personal imagery of who you believe yourself to be. And secondly, by implementing positive habits and behavioral traits to help manifest this change within the world. We don't make progress by accident, we succeed by consistently doing the things which will improve us little-by-little each day.

Again, if you are pursuing your ultimate purpose, this won't feel like work. However, I have found a productivity hack to help you along the way. Its a technique I use myself, in order to get more stuff done. Its the most important in my opinion, which is why I have dedicated the first section of this chapter entirely to it. The method I'm referring to is simply setting out to do a manageable amount of work each day, and doing it EVERYDAY. This may seem simple, but I assure you its powerful when performed over long periods of time.

When you aggregate these small workloads together, they really start to add up. I use this very technique when writing these books. I don't try to finish one in a month, or write 3000 words per day. That's a sure fire way to get burnt out and produce lower quality work. I have tried this before and end up re-editing all of what I've written anyway, effectively doubling the workload. Not clever.

Instead, I task myself with writing 1000 high quality words everyday. I might take Sunday off to really clear my mind, but you get the point. Writing a 1000 words 6 days a week for a year, adds up to a lot. Even if I take 2 weeks off for vacation, that's 300,000 words per year. Something which seems like a daunting task on first consideration, but eminently possible when employing this strategy.

The key is living in one day increments. To compartmentalize your life into 24 hour time frames by which you live by. This way you only deal with problems and issues as they arise. You also let your creative centers do their best work, as you are not clogging up the cognitive machinery with excess worry and doubt.

Dr. James Gilkey accurately describes this in his famous 1944 sermon titled "Gaining Emotional Poise". He discovered the idea whilst looking at an egg timer on his desk one day. He noticed that even though the sand would pass from the top to the bottom of the hour glass over several minutes, it would still only pass one grain at a time. Our lives are no different in this respect. Our problems all line up in single file, and we deal with them one-by-one as they come at us. It can't happen any other way. But we fret like we need to solve every potential issue, or cram all future activity into the hear and now.

If you can manage to change your thinking and working habits in this way I.e. by taking things more slowly, but much more consistently, you will be well on your way to greater progress in anything you are attempting to do. Your productivity will sky rocket, in addition to continually increasing your mental fortitude along with it. You are now the person who gets up and gets it done everyday, but saving enough in the tank to do the same tomorrow, that's the key.

That being said, there are some additional tips you can implement in order to form better habits. To be honest, I really dislike referring to psychological tools as "tips" or "secrets", as it suggests they are somehow shortcuts to success. This is the wrong way of looking at them. Yes they can help you immensely if you are willing to put the work in over time. But everything requires some level of effort to implement. So the following are some of these additional techniques which should help you along the way.

Priority Planning

The first of these strategies is to deal with work which requires your immediate attention first. If you are not working on a long term project, like writing 300,000 words per year, then its easy to become distracted with any number of things throughout the day. Therefore, good old fashioned planning is your friend here, in order to identify exactly what these tasks are first and foremost. Say for example you need to clear your inbox of any important emails before starting your daily work, then do this first thing without wasting further time. Allot an hour to answering these after breakfast for instance.

Pushing these tasks to a later point in the day will reduce their value, along with the likelihood they will get done. This seems like common sense, but I'm amazed at how many people can't even put this simple productivity habit into practice each day. I get each of my staff to identify and categorize all of their daily tasks in terms of what needs to be completed. Starting from the most critical, all the way down to the optional, then checking them off accordingly.

Most people struggle to admit this, but you will find that the things which make the biggest difference in your life, will often be the toughest too. They will be the things that you may least want to do. This wont always be the case I.e. the hardest task will garner the greatest payoff, but this 80/20 style thinking (where 20% of your work will create roughly 80% of your results) is a good principle to live by.

So after you have completed the immediate action and tough tasks, only then is it time to move onto the everyday activities. Tackling the tough or complicated duties first, when you have the most physical and mental energy to do so, ensures that you are left with enough time to finish up the easier ones which can be cleaned up with much less effort and brain power.

Simply list down what you NEED to achieve, and reward yourself with small treats as and when you complete them. This doesn't have to be anything major, just a piece of dark chocolate, or a fancy coffee perhaps. Just try to keep it as healthy as possible. On the flip side, punish yourself if you do not complete one of these critical tasks. This is more prevalent if you work for yourself within your own business for instance. I literally know people who would burn 100 dollar notes if they didn't get something done. I'm not suggesting you be that drastic, but you get the point.

I would donate 10 bucks to a random children's or animal charity that day. This may not seem like a lot, but I promise you, it begins to add up if you are continually missing activity deadlines. You quickly train yourself to get everything done, to prevent the consistent movement of money out of your bank account, albeit going to a good cause. You need to re-train your brain to automatically do the right thing. To strengthen the synapses and pathways which will lead to better results, whilst simultaneously downplaying acts which will do the opposite.

Rising Early

One of the easier ways I find to clear these immediate and critical tasks, is simply by getting up earlier in the morning. I know this won't be feasible for everyone, depending on what time you can go to sleep each night. However beating the sun up each day gives you a monumental head start on the rest of the world. I personally like to get a quick workout in, as well as clearing any pressing tasks before I hit the office. This entails not snoozing through the alarm clock at 5am, but jumping out of bed and attacking the day instead.

I'm not suggesting to continually reduce your sleep everyday. This is another way to sure fire burnout before long. Everyone requires varying degrees of rest for full physical and cognitive recovery. Some can get by with 5-6 hours sleep, others need 8-9 hours. What I have found over the years is that almost everyone can shave off an hour to their usual pattern, without serious ill effects on performance. If it requires retiring an hour early each night, or not binge watching that last Netflix episode, then so be it.

Avoid Multitasking

This is especially pertinent advice for men, but women could also do well to heed this message too. Multitasking is never a good idea as it reduces your focus on the task at hand, which ultimately reduces productivity for the most part. Pay attention to just one activity at a time and avoid the temptation to take on too many things at once. People presume they are being more efficient by being busy. But as we have seen already, this is a myth, and actually reduces productivity overall.

Remember that tasks are meant to be checked off one-by-one, and in order of importance. Once you have planned out this activity effectively, you job is to simply get your head down and work through them. Take each day as it comes and don't worry unduly about subsequent tasks. The will also get done in time. I promise you, by doing things properly from the outset, you will avoid any feelings of overwhelm whist getting everything done in the process.

PART 2: MENTAL STRENGTH - TECHNIQUES & PRACTICAL STRATEGIES TO NATURALLY ATTAIN IT

CHAPTER 5: FREEDOM FROM FEAR & SURVIVING STRESS

"Make sure your worst enemy doesn't live between your own two ears"

(Laird Hamilton)

Humans are undoubtedly the worrying animal, there's no getting away from it. If you employ the previously described strategy of living in one day segments, then you should dissipate much of this mental anguish from your life. If you need some additional help with living in the present moment, then take a look at my previous books advice regarding mindfulness and relaxation training. Much can be achieved with just a little meditation practice to center yourself each day.

If you are putting the right psychological principles into practice, then you should be on the right track to achieving true mental toughness anyway. As the feelings of fear and stress will naturally diminish as a by product of ever increasing productivity, as well as surrendering to the present moment. In this sense, we can learn much from the old practitioners of Stoicism. The Stoic forefathers such as Marcus Aurelius, Epictetus & Seneca, who taught us a great deal on how to deal with adversity.

Lessons From the Greeks

During his lifetime, Seneca faced a whole series of testing circumstances. In 41 BC, he was exiled to Corsica following accusations of adultery with the Emperors sister. He was allowed to return eight years later to become the tutor and adviser to then Emperor Nero, who had recently taken the throne. However, Nero proved to be one of the most tyrannical leaders in the history of the Empire, and Seneca was forced to continue in his advisory role, despite requests to be allowed to retire.

Even after this wish was granted, political intrigue continued to hound Seneca. He was accused of being involved in the Pisonian Conspiracy, the plot to assassinate Nero. Although he was undoubtedly innocent of the charges, he was compelled and ordered to commit suicide.

Throughout these turbulent periods of his life, Seneca always remained Stoic in his thinking. He did not simply study and write on the philosophy, but actively used it to navigate through the many ups and downs of life. To view the world with a rational mind and even emotional keel. As a result, he has become one of the most popular Stoic philosophers, with prominent and contemporary success figures promoting his works today.

Seneca has some of the most valid and timeless advice on dealing with stress and finding genuine happiness. The following is a series of snippets into his mind. A collection of quotations and explanations from his personal writings, which I find to be equally fascinating as they are insightful, especially when it comes to mental fortitude.

"Its better to laugh at life than to lament over it"

One of the main reasons we feel stressed is simply because we take things too seriously. We have to learn to look at situations in their proper context. Many times, what we see as an insurmountable problem, will look much less serious after a good night's sleep, or after letting some time pass. Remember that only one thing can be worked on at any one moment. So if you have to put something off until tomorrow, then do so without the feeling of resentment or guilt. And don't forget, we can always choose to laugh and release tension, it goes a long way.

"Hardships strengthen the mind as work does the body"

Although we commonly perceive stress as being bad and counterproductive, in some ways it can be a positive emotion, depending on how we deal with it. Being mentally strong means that you choose not to react with negative emotions to stressful situations, or let them engulf you entirely. Instead, we should always look at the situation objectively, to see how we can resolve it, and what we can learn from it. Seneca illustrated the value of dealing positively with stress during his exile. Although he must have felt intensely frustrated by the situation, he wrote comforting letters to his mother, rather than allowing himself to wallow in self-pity.

"The most powerful is the man who has himself under control"

Achieving mental stability and subsequent happiness, generally boils down to taking the reins of your own life. Taking control involves living with responsibility for your thoughts, and not allowing external events to affect you unduly. This is illustrated by the story of two friends, one of whom bought a newspaper every day, and said "good morning" to the store owner each time he did. But he never once received a reply. One day the man's friend asked, "Why do you keep greeting him if he never responds?" To which the man replied, "Why should I let him influence how I behave?"

The moral of the story is that we should do what is right for our own mental state. We shouldn't be concerned about what others are thinking, or how they are behaving. This puts us in the driving seat of our own destiny. When we feel like we are in control, we experience the kind of internal self-generated happiness which can not be matched by external validation from other people.

"There are more things to distress us than to hurt us, and we suffer more in apprehension than reality"

This is a big one. One of the most prominent sources of stress in peoples lives is the worry of things which MIGHT happen. We can all recall times when we have lost sleep over seemingly menial things. Will my new work colleagues like me? Will I fail my exam next week? What if bad weather ruins my garden party this weekend? The list is endless. However, continually fretting about things does us no good. It will only result in anxiety and unnecessary internal suffering, which in turn will affect our daily lives in a negative manner. Instead, and as always, we should focus only on the present moment, rather than obsessing about what might happen in the future.

"A man is only as miserable as he thinks he is"

Much of the time, we believe we would be happy if only we had more money, were better looking, or had a better job. But the truth is, happiness is a choice we make. People who have the things we aspire for, are often no more content than those who have less. In fact, its usually the opposite. There are plenty of poor people who are happy with what they have, no matter how modest it may seem to us.

Thus, happiness is a decision we make. It isn't something which you allow yourself to feel at some future point in time, when you have achieved some benchmark or goal. Life will always replace momentary success with additional problems and greater aspirations to strive for. Instead, we need to be happy first, then accomplishing the things we are working towards becomes exponentially easier and less stressful by very nature.

Its counterintuitive, but you have to relentlessly ensure you are thinking happy thoughts throughout each day to retain this positive disposition. That sounds like childlike and oversimplified advice, but I assure you it not only works, its the most efficient way of doing things. Much like self-compassion, happiness isn't a condition which requires prerequisites. Its a basic human right which is afforded to everyone.

Its the only state where genuine creativity and progress can happen. It has long been shown within psychological and medical studies, that every part of the human body works more efficiently when a person is happy. Eye sight, hearing, sensitivity to touch all improve. In addition to the minds problem solving ability, all of which are increased when mood is up-regulated. Being happy is therefore the most beneficial state to be in, not just from an ethical standpoint, but a mental health one too.

"As long as you are alive, continue learning how to live"

One of the biggest misconceptions people have about life, is that we stop learning the moment we finish formal education. However the truth is, this is simply where it begins. Life itself is the school which is always in session, so pay attention. There is always something new we can learn. All we have to do is adjust the way we look at situations to continually to pick up the lessons they are providing us.

One of the best ways a person can do this, is to learn from your mistakes. I have written in greater detail on the re-contextualization of set-backs and problems in previous editions. Very often, we do something that we wish we hadn't done. Instead of simply feeling bad about it, let us look at the situation objectively, and see what we could have done better, so that we won't make the same mistake again when confronted with a similar situation.

CHAPTER 6: GOAL SETTING SECRETS

Now that we've discussed some of the overriding principles which lead to greater degrees of mental toughness, such as dealing with fear and stress in the right way, as well as developing better habits. Its time to look at some practical ways to achieve this in your everyday life. The first of which is learning how to goal set properly. This concept very much compliments forming better habits, as it provides a blueprint to direct your day-to-day activities and behaviors in a more positive fashion. To keep you on the right track and out of trouble.

So many guru's and teachers get this wrong when it comes to goal setting in my opinion. They often state that goals should be extremely specific in terms of what a person desires I.e. certain brand of watch they want, particular corporate position or specific dollar amount of money in their bank account. But also in exactly what time-frame they wish to achieve it by I.e. in 3 months or by some set in stone date.

Whilst I agree with this thinking to some degree, especially with regards to shorter term goals. I believe its bad advice for the bigger things, the longer term targets you want to achieve. Let me tell you why. The human brain simply does not work in this way. The subconscious mind, which is ultimately responsible for providing the opportunities to actualize these achievements, does not work in specifics. It works in images, feelings and emotions instead.

In this sense, its far better to split goal setting up into two segments, the near term vs the long term, as both categorizes require a different mode of thinking to complete (conscious forebrain activity for the former, and subconscious "below the surface" activity for the latter). So lets begin by exploring the mechanisms by which we achieve these immediate milestones. But before we do, I want to point out that I find that there is much negative connotation towards the word "goal" in general. It smells of corporate jargon or self-help verbiage, which puts people off from ever jotting them down to begin with.

I typically find the word "target" better describes short term goals, as they are literal targets on a dartboard, which you can zero into with complete clarity. I also find that "project" has a more legitimate feel with regards to the loner term goals, as they encompass a larger body of work spanning many years in most cases. This word more accurately describes the way in which most people function (including myself) when striving for their ultimate life purpose. But lets start with the short stuff first.

Short Term Targets (1-3 months)

This is the appropriate time to be extremely specific. These are the tangible KPI style metrics you may encounter in a data entry job for instance. You may need to achieve certain benchmarks each day, week or month. This is desirable though, as you require short term targets to aim at to ensure maximum productivity. But also as a way to gauge short term progress. Similar to the dolphin analogy I mentioned previously, you should be setting up these target parameters before steamrolling for 1-3 months, and knocking them down as you go.

Have you ever wondered why its difficult to lose wait for no real reason? However, if you have to fit into that wedding dress in 6 weeks time, then all of a sudden it becomes that much easier. The reason is that the mind has a definite target to aim at, and a hardwired time-frame by which to achieve it by. This works for anything within a 90-day time period. I.e. getting fit for an upcoming triathlon, studying for an important exam and so on. The mind must conceive the goal clearly and believe it can be achieved. Then you can work towards it with enough focus and motivational juice to get you to the finish line.

This is why these goals SHOULD be quantifiable and time specific. The conscious and rational thinking centers of the brain can fully interpret these metrics and formulate exact A to B plans to achieve them. They also ensure the steady flow of small wins which are so important for your mental state. It induces the consistent release of feel good hormones and mood regulators such as serotonin & dopamine. However, this is where short term targets end in their effectiveness.

Long Term Projects (5-10 years)

When you are set on improving your own mental toughness, you have to really understand how the human mind works. This is especially true when dealing with longer time horizons. Larger and loftier life goals should be grandiose, they should be hyper-ambitious. Think of it like aiming for the horizon line, which is tough to reach in reality, as its a hypothetical point. That's fine though, as these purpose driven goals are so big and bold, they aren't meant to be hit. If you shoot for the stars, you'll likely hit the moon. But that's better then aiming for the moon and never leaving earths orbit. These aspirations will includes things like "becoming extremely wealthy" or "becoming a world class business leader" or "having a large and amazing family".

It's very difficult to quantify these things entirely. Exactly how much money constitutes being "extremely wealthy"? What position do you hold in what company? Exactly how many children, grandchildren are you going to have? The mind works with images and emotions regarding these instances. A far better strategy for longer term goals is to create a picture or movie in your mind about what these things would look like. How do you look and feel once you have achieved these things? What are you wearing? What car are you driving? How does your posture now look?

The mind cannot differentiate between past, present and future events with regards to imagery in the mind. If you attached enough shouldn't put time limits on these bigger goals.

I'm not giving you a green light to procrastinate forever before starting that life goal venture. You can always find excuses for not doing it, but in your heart of hearts, you'll know when you are ready. If you simply focus on the mental image of achieving it frequently enough, and then put in the consistent and required work on a daily basis, it will show up in your reality when its the perfect time for you. "Fall in love with the process, and the results will take care of themselves" as they say.

Again, attaining true mental strength has little to do with momentary bursts of motivation or courage. They help in some day-to-day instances to aid in overcoming minor obstacles. But the bigger and more substantial achievements are attained by making the subtle, but significant changes in your thinking over the long term. To improve your habits and set out goals to guide you accordingly. Then its about putting in the persistent work and application as always. This is the only way to ensure success, and not leave anything to chance.

CHAPTER 7: VISUALIZATION - MENTAL IMAGERY IS MENTAL TOUGHNESS

"Mental will is a muscle that needs exercise, just like the muscles of the body"

(Lynn Jennings)

So goal setting is one thing, its a great tool for certain circumstances such as the short terms targets we're aiming for. But as we've seen already, this process often falls short with regards to longer time frame life goals you have in stall for yourself. These take a different approach. They require another strategy to achieve them effectively, a method we have touched on in the previous chapter. What we really need here is a healthy and adequate dose of visualization, when its done in the right way.

It should be clear by now that I believe mental imagery to be a key factor in determining mental toughness. In fact, your own perception of yourself will dictate all of your subsequent behaviors, as well as what you'll get out of life. You can't do anything without a lot of psychological stress, when this image isn't aligned with the picture you have in your mind. This will largely be a consequence of your past programming and environmental experiences.

Do you view yourself as a strong person? If you do, then you most likely are, its as simple as that. Everything is linked to self-image, personality, drive, levels of happiness and so on. You will naturally behave in the way you see yourself. A smoker never quits smoking. They can't by very definition, because they're a smoker, its just what they do.

Yes they are addicted to the nicotine, but more importantly, they are addicted to the act of puffing on a little white stick several times a day. Its not until the person makes a conscious decision in their mind to become a non-smoker, can they effectively kick the habit. Only then is it possible to turn down the requests from colleagues for that mid-morning cigarette, as this action no longer fits with the mental perception of themselves. They are now a non-smoker, why would they go out an do that?

This is where your habits can really help. Ensuring that you consciously put the correct ones into practice each day in order to change this mental picture of yourself. Studies show that it takes at least 21 days for this to happen. Sticking with the smoker example. Its best to keep yourself busy during the times when you most often light up if you are indeed trying to quit, and replace the action of smoking with a more positive one. I have friends who now switch their morning cigarette with a fruit smoothie for instance. Not only is this a healthier alternative, it keeps their hands busy whilst preparing and blending the fruit.

Mental Imagery & Strength

But how can we apply this to intentionally becoming more mentally strong? This is simple when you think about it. Nobody reacts to things which occur to them in terms of the true facts about their circumstance. Instead, we react in a way which is in line with the mental picture we hold for ourselves. If you know you can handle a lot of discomfort before becoming distressed, then small things will just not bother you. Its a choice you make in your mind, which is no different from selecting what clothes you'll wear that day.

This is also why you hear mentally tough people state things like "Do not confuse me with the facts, I may often be wrong, but I'm never in doubt". This is because they have such a strong mental picture of their personality, that they believe they are right in any situation. It actually doesn't matter if they are or not, merely thinking this way guarantees they garner greater results by doing so. Of course you need some level of intellect to make this work, otherwise you will simply be exhibiting a classic case of the Dunning-Kruger effect.

If you are not aware of this principle, its simply a set of cognitive bias studies which illustrate that the most ignorant people in society, typically express the most superiority when it comes to their assumptions. Whilst the highest IQ individuals do the opposite, they downplay their arguments and express the most doubt with regards to their positions. Plato put it best when he stated "I am the wisest man alive, for I know one thing, and that is that I know nothing."

My advice is to have enough self-awareness to know your limits, but strong enough convictions to impose your will on a situation. This doesn't mean exacting any tyrannical control over others. Its just about being extremely steadfast with the positions you hold in your own mind. This is the only way to move forward with conviction, whilst eradicating any "analysis paralysis" which holds most people back from achieving anything of note. There's real power in just making a choice, whether that decision proves to be the correct one or not doesn't matter. You are now at the causal end of events, as opposed to only being subjected to their effects.

Real World Examples & Personal Practice

This not only works on a personal level, but a societal one as well. There are countless examples throughout human history where this mental threshold for something can be identified by the masses. When the bar has been set for certain achievements, which seem impossible to better. Each generation typically feels that they have reached the pinnacle of human performance, but then somebody, somewhere goes and smashes these expectations and a new standard is set.

One of the most famous of these instances involved Roger Banister, a British middle distance runner who competed in the

1950's. Before this time, nobody had ever run a mile in under 4 minutes. It was thought to be an impossible feat. However, in 1954 during an athletics meet in Oxford England, Banister did indeed complete the mile race in a sub-4 minute time. In fact, he only achieved it by six tenths of a second, with an exact finishing time of 3 minutes, 59.4 seconds. This slimmest of margins didn't matter though, the psychology barrier had been breached.

Suddenly the hoodoo was lifted and everyone in the world now recognized it could be done, and most importantly the other athletes. It took only 46 days for this record to be broken again, with sub-4 minute miles now being the norm today. Yes, the advances in exercise science will account for much of this progress. Improvements in sporting equipment/technology, as well as nutritional and training practices, help push the boundaries of human performance. But I submit to you that none of these aforementioned factors, even when aggregated together, have as much impact as the psychological importance of the human mindset.

You have to believe you can do something before you can do it. The body can't go where the mind hasn't been. You have to visualize yourself doing whatever it is you wish to achieve first and foremost. Then go about practicing each day with focus and persistent action until you attain it. This doesn't mean solely training in a physical sense too. Its been shown time and again that practising in the mind is just as effective as going through the "real life" motions when trying to improve at a given task.

There are countless studies such as basketball teams rehearsing the shooting of free throws in their minds over and over. When compared with other test groups who practiced just in the physical sense, there was no significant difference in performance when tested at the end of the trail. Archers, golfers, tennis players all use exactly the same visualization tactics to produce above average results, when it comes time to compete.

The top sporting psychologists typically get athletes to segment their training regimes into a 50/50 split. Half of the time sweating it out on the court or track, and the other half, mentally going through the motions. Remember that the mind experiences these instances in exactly the same way, if you envisage the process clearly enough. The emotional centers get activated equally in either case. In this sense, its a good way to practice performing under pressure, as well as strengthening the neural pathways for the actions in the mind.

If you think this sounds whacky, or like a waste of time, then I implore you to give it a try. Every time you get a quiet moment during the day, close you eyes and begin to visualize performing something which you are intentionally trying to improve at. This can be on the train to work, during a lunch break, or even sitting on the toilet. Really go through every minute detail regarding the action. See every sight, hear every sound and feel every emotion which arises. Paint the complete neurological map of the situation, and rehearse yourself performing the action perfectly, over and over again. I assure you, when it comes time to put your skills to the test, you'll be amazed with the results.

CHAPTER 8: TALKING TOOLS & CONVERSATIONAL SKILLS FOR GREATER GRIT

So having discussed the most important and overriding principles when it comes to assessing mental toughness. I wanted to finish up with one final factor, the tip of the iceberg when it comes to improving the strength of your psychological state. This includes the day-to-day interactions you will have with others. More specifically the talking tools and conversational skills you will need to develop, to ensure you are fully utilizing your new found mindset.

These are the persuasion techniques which can optimize your daily interactions, and guarantee you garner the most from them, or at least not continually get the worst end of the bargain. This advice isn't designed to be manipulative in anyway, it simply follows innate human tendencies. These strategies will help push things in your favor when you want them to, nothing more. So approach these practices with an open mind, and try to cultivate them within your daily interactions as much as possible.

1. Increasing Situational Awareness

As I've stated on many occasions, human beings are emotional creatures and we rarely see things as completely black or white. The naturally mentally strong do, but the majority of people live in the gray areas of their minds, especially when it comes to intense interactions and conversations. Its difficult for most folks to leave their emotions at the door in these situations. However, in my experience with persuading many throughout my academic and business life, this isn't actually necessary. You can't become robotic and discount your emotions entirely, so planning and accounting for what you'll be feeling is a much more realistic and beneficial strategy.

The mentally tough in society are able to emotionally empathize with others, without becoming personally attached to their situation. This typically involves becoming good at "small talk", developing a conversational style which allows you to build rapport by discussing benign topics like the weather, or your favorite sporting teams for instance. These are universal icebreakers in any language. They put people at ease as you have found some common ground whilst keeping things impersonal.

It has been studied and found that within high level business interactions, the participants who indulged in this harmless chatter, came to an amicable agreement 56% of the time. Whereas the people who kept the conversation strictly business, only secured one 40% of the time. You obviously need to use some common sense here, as there's a fine line between discussing pleasantries and boring the ear off someone!

But the most mentally strong can find this balance well. They build just enough harmony between the parties, before getting to the point of their argument. You can view it as setting the table so to speak. This can disarm the other person from challenging your positions too strongly (more on this later). People are much more likely to agree with you if they like you, and even more so if they view you as a friend. This will also involve mirroring the other person's mannerisms.

The truly psychologically stable are not only good talkers, but greater listeners. They are not simply trying to offer their position or waiting for their turn to talk. They listen intently in order to really pick up on what the other person is saying. Emulating what the other person is doing in terms of speaking style and physical gestures. When done correctly, they will likely pick up on this behaviour themselves, and start to subconsciously mimic you back.

Mirroring a person's mannerisms and behavior patterns is done naturally in all of the best interactions between humans, and for good reason. It builds empathy and a bonding that makes both parties feel connected, at ease, and much more likely to give concessions from their side. It has been observed time and again that top negotiators who mimicked their opponent, almost always secure a better outcome as a result.

That is not to say you can give tacit approval to others. This is important to learn for those with weak dispositions. If somebody is explaining something to which they do not agree with, they will commonly just nod their head or say nothing at all. This indicates to the other person, and any one else in the room, that they agree with their position by default. Or they certainly do not disagree enough to pull them up on what they are saying. This is how "BS" is perpetuated, (for want of a better term), by those who are not strong enough to call it out when its needed. Yes build empathy and rapport to begin with, but don't be afraid to break it if something really runs counter to your morals.

2. Not Fearing "No"

"A "No" uttered from the deepest conviction is better than a "Yes" merely uttered to please, or even worse, to avoid trouble"

(Mahatma Gandhi)

If you've read the old school literature on negotiation tactics, this will seem like counterintuitive advice. But not fearing the word "no" can be of great benefit to you. It's typically stated that you should be escalating a line of questioning to get a "Yes" at the end of the interaction. Or attempt to get an incremental ladder of "Yes's". The theory is that it puts the person in an agreeable state of mind, and more likely to eventually come around to your way of thinking. Although in reality, this is often seen as an obvious attempt to manipulate the person into something they do not want to do. They anticipate this trap and usually break the line of questioning. Its commonly referred to as "cornering" in psychology circles.

The next time you are negotiating with a client or colleague, ask questions that allow them to express their stance on the issue so they feel more secure and in control. This will give them the opportunity to decline, and make them feel in control. It will also provide them a sense of security that will greatly smooth the path through the reminder of the interaction if done correctly. So don't be afraid of the word "No". Its far more beneficial and time conserving then getting a long line of maybes…

3. Be More Agreeable

This will also seem to run counter to having a strong mindset, as well as my previous two points on not giving tacit approval or fearing the word "No". But being more agreeable is really about being less strident with your position, and surrendering to the situation. This gives you the most power to manoeuvre. If you are able to truly empathize with another person's grievances, it gets them onside and in a less defensive posture. It has to be done in a genuine manner of course, and not when the suggestion is against your deep help values. But it can be very effective when applied in many of the everyday life and business settings you'll find yourself in.

The next time somebody states something like "I feel this isn't fair on me". Just reply with "I agree, lets figure out a way that everybody can win here". This is really only a small sound bite on your part, but will have a big payoff in terms of the persons emotional response when done correctly. It again emphasizes a connection, harmony and reminds the person that you share empathy with their position, and not just out for getting what you want from the interaction.

Try it the next time anybody gives you the slightest objection to something, even if it's the way you made their coffee. Just say "I agree" and watch the reaction you receive. The person's guard immediately drops as it's a surprising thing for somebody to do so readily. It doesn't mean that you are backing down, just disarming the person of any psychological resistance to your next move/statement, and initiates the urge within them to reciprocate in an agreeable way.

It communicates strength of character, that you are willing to explore the possibilities, that you won't be too adversely affected if things don't entirely go your way. It demonstrates a calmness to your demeanour, and a maturity in your behavior. On the other hand, weak and petty people continually have to get what they want in a childlike fashion. The key is to be strong in your convictions, but open to the outcomes. Guiding in your interactions, but surrendering to the ultimate outcome.

CONCLUSION

"Mental toughness is many things. Its humility, as it behooves us all to remember that simplicity is the sign of greatness, and meekness is the sign of true strength"

(Vince Lombardi)

If you have found the advice contained within this book, to run counter to what you commonly held true for developing mental strength, than I have done my job. Just think about it for a second. How far has the traditional way of doing things got you up until this point? Not where you want to be right? I say this not to provoke, but to illustrate what is possible when following another route. A more up to date path. We don't live in a world where grinding physical work predominately wins the day. We live in a time where proper thinking does. When the correct psychological strategies are implemented in the right manner.

Most people get entrenched in their way of doing things. When they come up against some form of opposition, they double down on what wasn't working in the first place. This is rarely effective though, as it requires more effort in a physical sense, but is lazy in a mental one. Instead, try some of the counterintuitive strategies I've mentioned in the preceding chapters. Often the most progress can be made by pulling in the opposite direction for a time. To go against the grain and surrender to the situation. Most people can't do this as it looks like weakness, but is in fact, genuine strength.

This is not to say you should act helpless or like a victim. I'm not a hugely religious person, although I do think there is some truth to the Old Testament metaphors and allegories in the Christian Bible. But there's certainly a line in the New Testament which always bothered me. Its from the Sermon on the Mount, when Jesus states "Blessed are the meek: for they shall inherit the earth". This very much sounds like the weak, harmless, and timid will eventually come out on top. But how can this be?

From everything we've been commonly told up until this point, it takes the opposite. It requires strength and a robustness in our approach to getting things done. "Good things come to those who wait, but only whats left from those who hustle" is more like it. But when you dig a little deeper into the Greek and Hebrew roots of the word "meek", you start to understand what is really being said here. What its actually describing is that "those who have weapons and know how to use them, but choose to keep the sheathed" will eventually gain everything.

In a psychological sense, this now fits perfectly with what I'm getting at, and what our real world observations indicate. It takes a wise and strong character to prosper, someone who has the potential to be dangerous, but chooses not to be. Someone who is mentally strong, but chooses to exercise restraint. Those who understand that they can't control everything in their environment, only their own emotions and reactions to things. But in truth, that's all that matters, as that's all you can effect.

Then you can be the role model to yourself and others, the person the less fortunate look up to. That is the true nature of mental toughness. Being steadfast when its needed, but ultimately surrendering to everything, and not sweating the small stuff. "A man is judged by the size of the things which bother him" is often stated, and I couldn't agree more. That literally might be the most accurate way to sum up true mental strength.

But it takes a little contemplation, work and training first. Its about making steady progress. Life has a habit of putting Goliath in your way, but only when you are ready to find the David within you. If you put a frog in a pan of room temperature water, and slowly increase the heat. It wont know what is happening, until it eventually boils and dies. The same thing happens to us throughout life, but we don't die, we just get stronger. We just become better equipped to deal with hardships.

Hopefully I have laid out some principles and strategies to help you do just that. To give you a different perspective on how you can view the world. To ensure you naturally become more stable in your thinking by default, rather than enduring what seems like an endless and grinding struggle. Its a much more efficient option I can assure you. It will almost feel like a magic when you get it right.

BONUS CHAPTERS

(From 'Self-Esteem: A Psychologist's Guide')

CHAPTER 5: DEVELOPING BETTER THINKING PATTERNS

"Take care how you speak to yourself, because you are listening"

(Anonymous)

It's extremely important to be vigilant with regards to your thoughts and feelings when initially attempting to raise your overall levels of self-esteem. To become an emotionally stable individual, you have to be aware of what is going on inside of you at all times. There is no right or wrong assumptions to be made to begin with. Like everyone else, your emotions will be a mixture of irrational reactions by and large.

Humans typically elicit emotional responses easily and swiftly in almost every situation, and suppressing them is a tough task. But that's OK. This is just the start. It's about identification and recognition of these feelings to begin with. Especially when they are negative in nature regarding your personality or physical traits, as they can so easily lead to negative spirals of thinking.

This is the brains default position. Humans are very much hardwired to focus on the negative. We zero in on the potential dangers we face, as it was so important to do so from an evolutionary standpoint. Our survival was dependant on directing urgent attention towards negative outcomes. If you attributed the rustling in the bushes to the movements of a saber-toothed tiger, then you had time to react. If you dismissed it as the wind, and it wasn't, then you were removed from the gene pool.

It's officially known as the "Negativity Bias" to psychologists. It explains how we inherently focus on the unpleasant thoughts and emotions such as harmful and traumatic events. This is true even when we are presented with an equal amount of neutral or positive situations. Negative factors have a much greater and disproportionate effect on a persons psychological state. It takes 5-7 positive thoughts, just to balance out a single negative emotion!

In this sense, we have a tendency to profess over the downsides we view within ourselves. Over thinking these traits is certainly not a wise thing to do. If you are not careful you can get trapped in your own mind. This is especially relevant when contemplating undesirable attributes.

In fact, a person with genuinely high levels of self-esteem, will learn to quiet the mind for the majority of the day. They will use their cognitive ability wisely, and simply to plan the necessary tasks they have to complete. To organize their routines before getting back to relative calm and stillness of thought. They largely use the brain for what it is, a tool at their disposal.

The brain is undoubtedly a complex organ. Its required to perform an incredible number of calculations every second, even during mundane tasks like guiding the body for movement in simple motor skills, all the way up to making crucial and complex decisions in real time. The brain undertakes millions of these interconnected decisions every single day, thereby making it one of the most powerful pieces of biological machinery we have.

So it should be used wisely and with care, especially when it comes to developing thought patterns and habits which ultimately dictate our daily behaviors and thinking patterns. It does this in an attempt to optimize a person's day-to-day movements and thought processes, but these short cuts aren't always beneficial.

The formation of these pathways is known as neuroplasticity. Neurology has intrigued scientists & psychologists greatly over the past two centuries. From the Classical Conditioning described by Pavlov and John Watson, to the Operant Conditioning of B. F Skinner. Each presented theories which described how the human brain works and learns.

Its no secret that a person's daily habits and thinking routines will ultimately dictate how they view themselves. However habits are impartial, they will either help a person attain their desired results, or they will ensure they continue getting the average/poor results they have always gotten. As Dr Richards Bandler frequently points out "Brains aren't designed to get results; they just go in directions".

So how can we use this knowledge to help improve our self-esteem an overall mental state? In reality, its simply a case of learning your

ABC's I.e. learning the sequence of the Antecedent, Behavior and Consequence. I have explained these concepts in greater detail within previous books, so I'll just stick to the technique here so you can implement it when it comes to negative self-talk.

Thought Pattern Interrupts

The idea is to disrupt a negative thought pattern as early on in the cycle or sequence as possible, more specifically between the trigger and operation phase. Regardless, it must be completed before the testing phase of the condition, to say that you must disrupt it before the mind tries to test the original assumption, otherwise any attempt to break the sequence will be of little use as the pattern is almost completed.

The pattern interrupts aren't difficult to implement and its simply about stopping your train of thought and thinking about something different. It's a case of "butting in" on your own thought process and the conversation occurring within your own head. You are simply trying to change the direction of the mind and reprogram it as you do. You are not removing the old pattern per se, but rather redirecting around it.

To use an example from an earlier chapter regarding accomplishments. If you wish to stop viewing others as continually better than yourself. You need to stop focusing on THEIR results, but rather focus on YOURS instead. You need to implement a thought pattern interrupt when you feel yourself becoming conscious of the gap in your perceived abilities. The following steps can help greatly with this:

1. Not Holding Back

The aim is to ensure the interrupt is as big and bold as possible. If there is one mistake I see from people who try this method, is that they are too weak with their disrupting action, and it isn't enough to fully divert their thinking. This is especially true regarding a long term, entrenched belief or pattern of thought which they are trying to break I.e. I'm not as good as everyone else. Try a loud clap of the hands or harsh cough whenever you feel this emotion as a significant interrupt.

2. Time it Correctly

You need to ensure you catch the "trigger phase" as accurately as you can, as it will be key to identifying when you need to employ the pattern disrupt. In essence, this should be directly after the original thought is spotted.

This stimulus/response window is typically a very short period of time. So you really have to be a keen observant throughout the day to catch them when they do occur. This can often be a thought or memory which pops into the mind which starts the negative cycle of thinking.

If you allow it to continue, your emotions and physiology will start to change. At this point it will be too late. You have to become proficient at catching it right before this transition takes place I.e. immediately following the trigger thought/memory, and replace your momentary behavior to a more positive one.

3. Rinse & Repeat

Simply catching the cycle once will not be enough for most entrenched poorly held beliefs. The real payoff comes from repeating this cycle over and over until the new thinking pattern becomes habitual, and you start to see the results you are looking for I.e. a more realistic and positive outlook towards yourself.

So ensure you perform whatever interrupt you have chosen until it becomes second nature to you, until you no longer have to think about it. You have to bring the skill into the "Unconscious Competence" phase when performing it. That is when the new direction of thought and subsequent behavior will properly take hold.

This general approach was taken from hypnotherapists such as Milton Erickson who used pattern interrupts to disrupt the waking thinking patterns of their participants. They would lead a persons inner monologue down a familiar path before disrupting the line of questioning, leaving the persons unconscious mind waiting for the logical next step of the pattern, but it never comes. This can be a powerful enough confusion of the mind which puts a certain percentage of the population into a hypnotic trance.

You are not attempting to go this far with yourself, and it's almost impossible to do it on your own. However the general thought pattern interrupt is designed to work along the same lines. But this time to disrupt a familiar negative thought pattern and replace it with a positive more beneficial one.

Understanding that you will almost certainty be running negative and automatic negative thinking patterns is half of the battle. Breaking them is quite another fight altogether. It requires tools such as thought pattern interrupts to ensure newer and more positive upgrades are embedded into your psyche. So make sure you are cognizant of putting this effective cognitive trick into practice throughout the day as much as you can.

CHAPTER 6: THE BENEFITS OF CATASTROPHIZING

"A women is like a tea bag, you never know how strong she is until she gets in hot water"

(Eleanor Roosevelt)

In the previous chapter we discussed the importance of not letting negative thinking patterns remain in your mind indefinitely. Most of these patterns are now so ingrained into the synapses of the brain, they pretty much run on autopilot each day. This is why its so important to consciously break them. However, there is one instance where this catastrophizing behaviour can actually be beneficial.

I'll admit this is more of a confidence boosting exercise, rather than a complete self-esteem overhaul. In truth, its simply a strategy which can put your mind at ease for a multitude of situations. In this sense, I find it extremely useful for building ones own self-esteem as a by product. This is a trick to ultimately worry less. If you achieve this, you will just find yourself acting in a more harmonious and beneficial manner by proxy.

As we have already seen, most people use this concept of catastrophizing in the wrong way. They easily enter negative thinking spirals by default, which is why they are so difficult to avoid. If you are not careful, just the slightest misconception or negative connotation towards an event, can have you extrapolating out near disastrous outcomes in no time. My aim for this chapter is to show you how to use this natural tendency to your benefit.

This requires taking these negative trains of thought to their natural conclusion. You are already thinking of every bad outcome to begin with, so going one step further is not too much to ask. Let me give you an example. When I was initially starting up my consulting business, I had to employ a handful of staff to take care of all admin and house keeping tasks. This freed me up to deal with existing clients, as well as perform business development activities in order to attract new ones.

I would constantly worry about how I was going to make payroll each month, even though I knew we had several months of capital allocated to cover such costs. My main worry though, was actually the thought of one of my staff quitting, and leaving me with nobody to invoice my clients. Worst still, what if they took all of this sensitive information to a rival company and left me with nothing?

One day I decided that enough was enough and sat down to really think this situation through. I intimately explored every detail of this worst case scenario and lived out each outcome in my mind.

I realized that in such a circumstance, I would simply have to find someone new, and start from scratch finding new clients all over again. This would give me the opportunity to find a new rock star employee as well as sharpen my sales skills. This actually started to seem quite an attractive situation.

But in reality, I came to the conclusion that all I really needed to do was get my staff to sign NDA's and client poaching clauses, as well as systematize their work & I'd be protected. Sure enough, within 6 months of doing this, my secretary quit to work for another company agreeing to keep all client information confidential. I then hired another lady to do the job and she learnt the systems and procedures within a week.

Nothing is ever as bad as it seems to be, or we project that its going to be. In fact, once you go through this worst case planning exercise, anything less than a disaster seems like a win. This greatly increases a persons confidence in their day-to-day lives, allowing them to move forward without all of the mental anguish which once held them back.

Remember its always beneficial to keep the old Zen Master in mind. To remind yourself of the old Taoist story of the farmer and his son. If you do not know it, the fable goes something like this:

There once was an old farmer who worked his crops with the aid of a trusty horse. One day the horse ran away, and the villagers lamented "What bad luck that is!".

The Zen master simply replied "We'll see".

The following day the horse returns, bringing with it three additional wild horses. To which the villagers cheered "How wonderful!".

The Zen master once again replied "We'll see".

A week later the farmer gives one of the horses to his son as a gift on his sixteenth birthday. The villagers reply, "Oh, how lovely, the boy got a horse!"

The Zen master says, "We'll see."

A few days later the boy gets thrown off the horse and breaks his leg. All of the villagers again lament, "How terrible!"

The Zen master replies, "We'll see."

The village is then visited by military officers who draft all the young men to go fight in the war. But the boy can't go as his leg is in a cast. The villagers say, "How lucky that is!"

The Zen master says, (you guessed it) "We'll see…."

MENTAL TOUGHNESS

This story automatically springs to mind whenever I view a situation as either being very good or bad. It's another pattern interrupt I've imprinted into my own thinking over the years. The words "We'll see" naturally pop into my mind whenever I feel a negative thinking spiral begins to occur.

Its of course good to keep an even keel when it comes to viewing extreme situations as inherently negative or positive. But most critical when catastrophizing events in your mind. Sit down and analyze these instances and plan for the worst. If you experience them in your head first, you will become much less afraid of them playing out in your physical reality.

You may even become disappointed if they don't! Hardships and troubles are the only true way to grow our characters and expand our comfort zones. Dealing with these instances in our minds and perhaps in "real life" is therefore the stepping stones to a stronger resolve, and ultimately a better life.

Printed in Poland
by Amazon Fulfillment
Poland Sp. z o.o., Wrocław